Praise for My Radar Data Knows Its Thing

With each poem that begins with his namesake's classic line, Lytton Smith's chapbook tests the limits of language just as it tests the limits of human relationships. Words hold us together even when we're questioning their validity. Our linguistic (and so our human) scale has just gotten bigger and bolder.

-Anthony Caleshu

Praise for Lytton Smith

Lytton Smith shows one of the directions contemporary poetry should be headed.

-David Herd

Though he knows so much, because he knows so much, being so restlessly at study, Lytton Smith can't help but celebrate seeing.

-Fred Moten

Lytton Smith's work opens a space for breath and inquiry in between the spectacle and its consequences [...] (gorgeously) records borders rather than insisting communication can abolish them.

-Laura Mullen

Keep your eyes peeled for this poet.

-Kevin Young

[a] poet of visionary intensity and bedeviled diction.

-Terrance Hayes

My Radar Data
Knows Its Thing

For permission requests, email foundlingszine@gmail.com.

www.foundlingsmagazine.com

Printed in the United States of America

First Edition

ISBN: 978-0-9997539-1-0

FOUNDLINGS PRESS

"It was a dark and stormy night;"

—Edward Bulwer-Lytton
opening to *Paul Clifford* (1830)

[It was a dark and stormy night;
but who remembers] 51 54

[It was a dark and stormy night.
We keep returning here, as if] 48

[It was a dark and stormy night.
Night an approximation] 34

[It was in the absence of light] 26

TABLE OF CONTENTS

It was a dark and stormy night. It was rainy weather
and the limits of our language were our weather.

When you said, soft as eggshell brought to powder,
Thing is, I didn't want this, it brought to mind

all the tugboats I couldn't send back, couldn't
offshore, couldn't make lead their galleon liners

out to breakwater, out from breakwater to ocean
shelf, from ocean shelf to where the world's recycling

gathers itself the smallest island, a set of archipelagos,
what the world's done and won't take back, or can't—

Nut brittle, back scrubber, the hexagonal panels peeled
from soccer balls, all milling an eddy. What I'd known

we didn't want but had forgotten, like the in-joke
in which we were famous meteorologists, inventing

weather systems and cloud formations almost at will.

And then to realise the world we'd made wasn't the one

each of us thought the other thought we were making,
the way an occluded front forms as a cold front overtakes

a warmer. When you said, There I was, outside myself, I saw
tugboats resolutely bringing in all the things I'd harboured

too long without knowing.

It was a dark and stormy night and in the message
that somehow records on tape I missed your voice
at first. The magnetic principle implies a burred
technology, less residue than active attachment.

The radar sighs and retracts. Nothing to be done
now sound has lost its density, gone byte-size.
The data piles in reams in the corner, hunkers
for the nights to come. The morse code I light

your way with—my bedroom bulb—I offer
without recourse to the manual. Still light
peters out long before where you are. The rain
and wind give way to the marine layer. Sound

and light in the distance unrecorded. A glass
against a wall and hearing only my own blood.

It was a dark and stormy night; my radar had lost all sense of the approaching. My brother on the phone talked of the descent into Santos Dumont Airport, the fuselage dropping itself into cloud and dropping itself into cloud and the windows cowled with the soft grey of dirty wool and the fuselage dropping and landed without ever seeing the sky, the skyline, the streets approaching, the runway. What if that's how it's all happening, so that we don't know whether we've started our descent or are still circling? What's really cool is this home radar system tracks aircraft within five hundred miles of where we live (and more). It scans transponder codes, cycles incoming and outward-bound. (Except for when its uninflected off-black screen finds nothing out there moving, and I can almost hear the sinewy swivel of my neck's upper vertebrae as my head turns the way a satellite might list for frequency. That muscular torque to the mechanical, an unceasing movement towards what might be out there that sometimes passes for nothing but listlessness, my face passing between the windows of this house, left to right to left to right towards what I can't see there.)

It was a dark and stormy night and I was ghoulish in the thrown
glow of the radar's data.

I'd forgone window and roof as measures, stopped trusting the
subjectivities of our linguistic scale.

I'd come to lack my own body as antenna and instrument of the
atmospheric and what then.

What the radar's concentrics synthesise is the most detectable or
least missable of stimuli—each blip indexing the
incoming event, retreating act, some body in satellite.

E.g. hulled submersible. E.g. stricken tanker. E.g. the bewildered
bovine herd pulled simultaneously to the safety on
either side of the highway. E.g. a kite's gyroscopic
designs. E.g. all of memory reappearing at once.

Hunched at the radar I learn again to recognise the build of
moisture in my nostrils, promised rain. I teach myself to
predict the trajectory of the smallest of the blips.

What the data has to tell me I'm not yet ready to tell you. Not
for its content but for its distance. (What I'd tell by
forest fire I wouldn't by semaphore.)

And as I watch the luminescence redouble on the display, I
wonder if anyone's invented weather as a means of
communication.

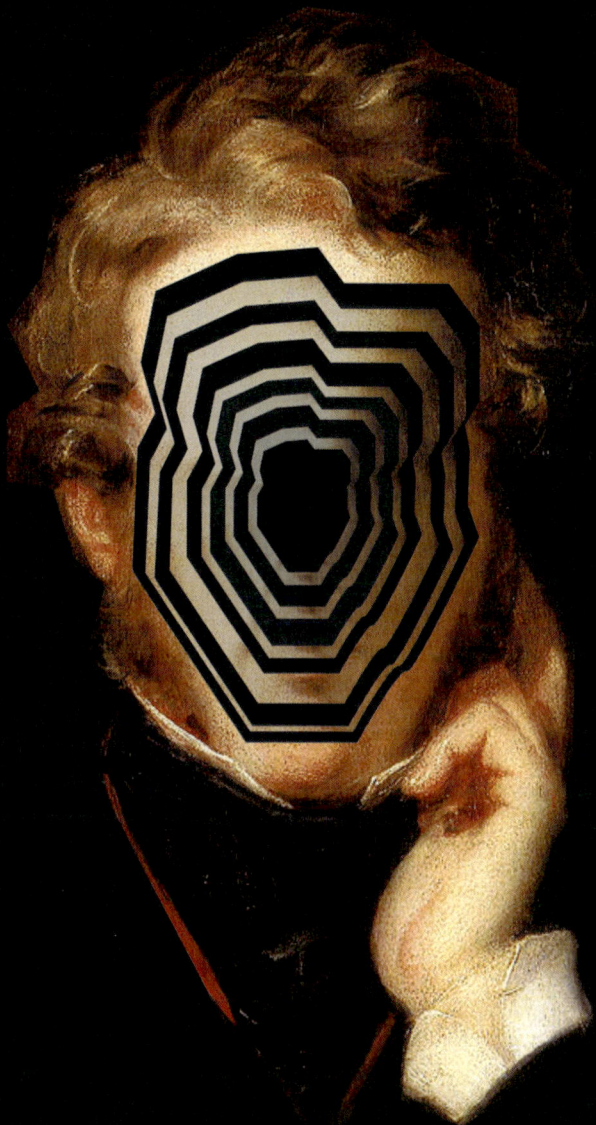

It was a dark
and stormy night.

Pathetic fallacy: if
blue won't gunpowder

or gentian without
the lit catalyst—

the troublesomeness
of the metaphysicians—

where does that leave
our phrase? Burrowed

into the couch
the impression

of your having left.
The eggshells waiting

grinding and binding
into slaked lime, brushing

into whitewash. With
the outer covered over

the inward twinges
towards eureka.

It was a dark and stormy night—stop me if you've heard this one before—and the instruments in disagreement, the barometer's careful measure inflecting the AM radio's rustled frequency. Within our lifespan the climate changes daily, or how the seasons have disappeared once. This April winter the hedgehogs slept on into their hunger, waiting for a warmth that never eased them into forage. Their slumbered, shivered bodies feeding on stored carbohydrates until they were left with nothing but sleep. And yet we talk of quickening, a hand to the rib from inside the body. And yet we talk of geodesic homes, of self-build, of the startled edge of an 18th century building around which an urban fox in the road, staring you down, without threat, as if to say, *Yes, here I am.* I keep bringing the past into the present: it was a dark and stormy night, I begin, and here we are, looking back hardly over our shoulders as footfall ticks us forward.

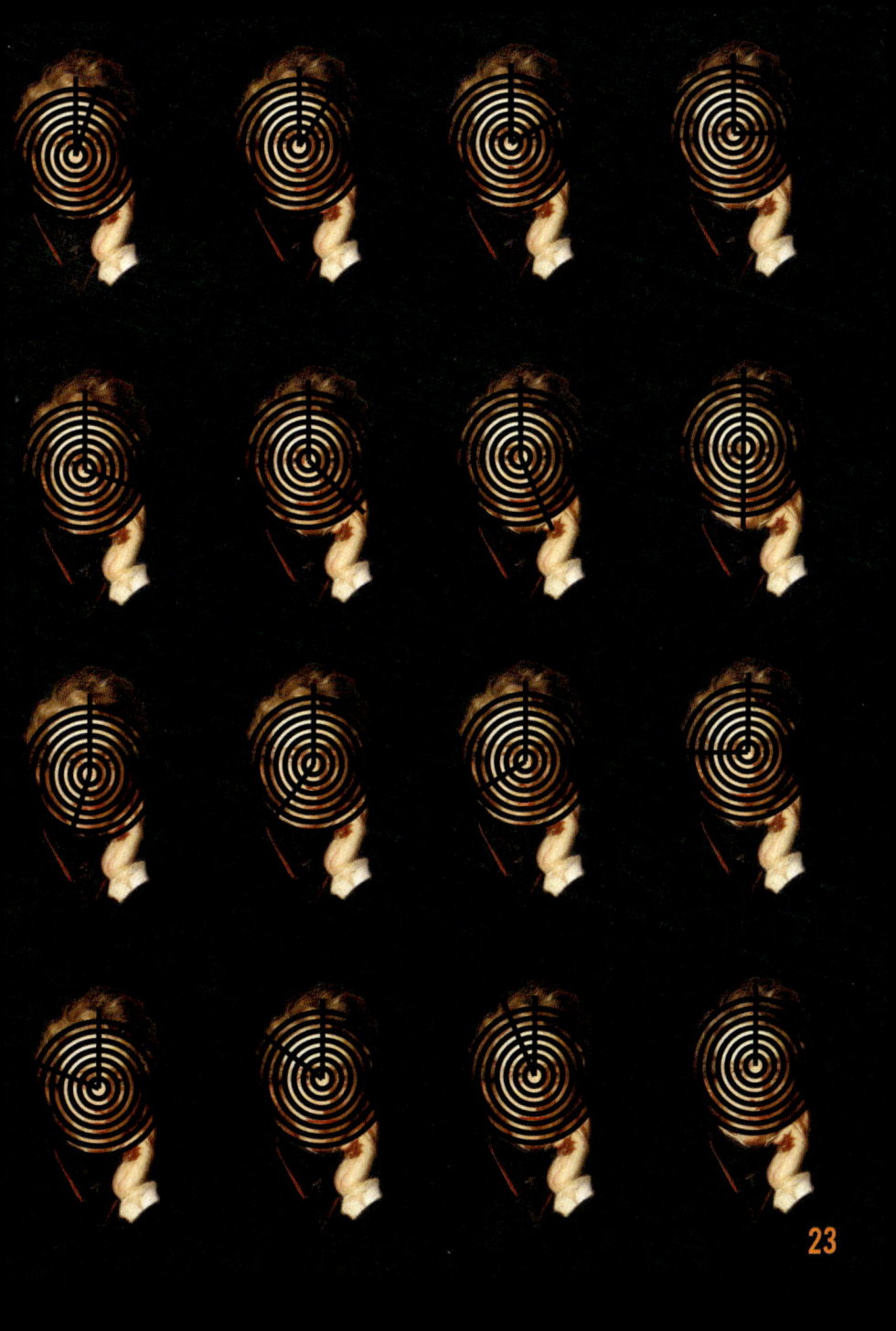

It is a dark and stormy night always
in the cartoon strip where the way
the world ends each day
doesn't govern its next appearance.

Picture this: not the roof of a kennel
but the palette of the mouth, not
the lightbulb above the homicidal cat's
head but the tip of a tongue pulled up

in the half-pause before enunciation.
In the next frame the sound made
is political, its frequency scanning
the conched trumpets of several ears.

It was in the absence of light
as when near new moon and
no moonlight; as when a part

of a picture is in shadow (as
opposed to a light); as when
in the condition of being

hidden from view, obscure,
or unknown—in concealment,
or else without knowledge

as regards to some particular;
and of the weather, season,
air, sky, sea, etc., characterized

by tempest; in times, events,
circumstances etc. subject to
tempers; inflamed, indicative,

predictive, or symbolic of
strife (harbinger of coming
trouble)—a period of darkness

occurring between one day &
the next during which a place
receives no light from the sun,

and what if it is all behind us?
I no longer fear the rain will
never end, but doubt our ability

to return to what lies passed.
On the radar, a photopresent
scraggle of interference, as if

the data is trying to pretend
something's out there where
everything is lost.

It was a dark and stormy night, by which I mean watching

the climatological present itself in the ways physics wishes—

collided front, atmospheric shift, precipitate—and learning

the instruments and practices necessary to its reading:

in the sleight of English country roads headbeams smuggle

villages into shape while I'm wondering what I've enabled

you into. Or: then, that night, downpour registered against

a scale of sound on the roofing, cycling the frequencies

for where the atmosphere prickles the signal crossing over.

Writing back to you from the world's other side I learned

I had missed all the things poised in the half-breath before

falling. The cartoon anvil. The villain's shadow. The penny

dropping. No longer owning the books you inscribed to me

nor having deliberately decided to discard them either

I am here watching climatology's showiest depression effects.

It was a- but this you know. Time passes
and I come to think it was not words held

us together but the improvised tactics
of an astroturf arena. Fluent into space,

man management, what's known as reading
the game, this somatic way we learned

each other's language, and I yours, yielding
an inherited *football* for the percussions

of *soccer*. How we kept playing late into
the floodlights, the pitch inch-thick

with rain that wouldn't sluice. How we
kept playing long into the absence

of those who should have been there. How
I don't know a better way to say I miss you

than a ball arced from my keeper's arms—
a flash of yellow jersey—up front to where

I hope you are waiting to trap, to swivel,
to flick on, the movement continuing—

It was a dark and stormy night. Night an approximation:
somewhere in the halls of aurality *nox* shifts its vocables
closer to *nacht*, the palette rises the pitch of inside vowel,
and what we're left with is night, nightingale, night terrors,

time of storms, of coming to terms with a scale of weather
we've only language for: at *gale*, some cars veer on roads,
at storm (*whole gale*), shingles in poor condition peel off roofs.
By storm I don't mean metaphor. I mean a thing arrivant

and conjunctive, additional to the state we're used to
and shifting its weathering. Beyond this lies the removal
of the way of life we've abraded into—river home, sun
rarely, coastal-minded—and we're holding here against

its chance appearance. In a box, coiled catgut for stringing
an instrument's neck: like weather, silent until stretched
to its resonance. History as that return from the past
we've not found a use for yet. That we're not meant to.

Asked you all how it was when it was last
a dark and stormy night; our survey said
offglow thrown from a laptop screen, said
head down into the visual display unit, said
moongone, said how the lights from the town
at the end of the ride could have been a fire
burning the homes we were cycling to, said
we kept playing the game as the puddles iced
in the head-on beams of the floodlights, said
it was in a play and the mariners kept slipping.

Out here, I copy you. We've never been more different
nor more differently arranged. A leg thrown over
an armrest in a state potato-rife. A love affair re-ending
in a winter strict with outdoor passes. Alone
in another themed restaurant—literary cocktails &
fabulous allusions at Knebworth—time slipping
like a gear chain. How I ride out in a wind which almost
broadsides me into an ocean that could in theory fetch
me back. I can't explain to you who aren't even there.

This has nothing to do with the night, with the dark, or storms
but today they're tearing down the Village pub where we said

three words about love. They're tearing down the iconic green
gas station too, the rectangle of sky above that opens like a rhombus.

If they build over a building in a city we've left, does the building
disappear? I hear again the wind again, in the construction site,

footloose in the rubble before the office block. I was wrong:
This is how an island disappears, as the square acre we made

our footholding—the used bookstore housing half our words,
the stumbled-upon pub's dented hardwood an ostensible time capsule—

gets landscaped, and when we return there isn't anywhere to return.
Up the road, up from where the gridlock somehow rolls itself forward,

the filmic Jewish deli sighs and is gone. In my memory this feels
silent, the way I can't catch my breath, a panicked shut-valve,

just yellow cabs against green husting against redbrick tenements and
as it's about to go I hear the caught lungwork of six words about love.

This has nothing to do with the night, with the dark, or storms,
the stumbled-upon pub's dented hardwood, an ostensible time capsule.

Footloose in the rubble before the office block I was wrong.
Disappear I hear again the wind again, in the construction site,

the gas station too, the rectangle of sky above that opens like a rhombus.
The filmic Jewish deli sighs and is gone. In my memory this feels

three words about love. They're tearing down the iconic green
but today they're tearing down the Village pub where we said

If they build over a building in a city we've left, is there a building?
This is how an island disappears, the square acre we made

up the road from where the gridlock somehow rolls itself forward
toward yellow cabs against green husting against redbrick tenements and

gets landscaped. And when we return there isn't anywhere to return.
As we're about to go I hear the caught lungwork of six words about love,

our footholding—the used bookstore housing half our words—
gone silent, the way I can't catch my breath, a panicked shut-valve.

As we're about to go I hear the caught lungwork of three words about love.
But today they're tearing down the Village pub where we said

(the gas station too, the rectangle of sky above that opens like a rhombus)
This is how an island disappears, the square acre we made.

This has nothing to do with the night, with the dark, or storms.
Disappearing, I hear again the wind again, in the construction site,

get landscaped, and when we return there isn't anywhere to return.
Six words about love: they're tearing down the iconic green

they built over a building in a city we've left, and is that building,
the stumbled-upon pub, its dented hardwood, an ostensible time capsule,

our footholding? The used bookstore housing half our words gone
silent, the way I can't catch my breath, that panicked shut-valve.

Up the road, up from where the gridlock somehow rolls itself forward,
footloose in the rubble before the office block, I was wrong:

just yellow cabs against green husting against redbrick tenements and
the filmic Jewish deli sighing, gone. In my memory this feels

footloose in the rubble before the office block. I was wrong:
this has nothing to do with the night, with the dark, or storms.

The filmic Jewish deli sighs and is gone. In my memory this feels
as it's about to go. I hear the caught lungwork of three words about love

if they build over a building in a city we've left. The building
up the road, up from where the gridlock somehow rolls itself forward,

gets landscaped, and when we return there isn't anywhere to return,
just yellow cabs against green husting against redbrick tenements and

six words about love. They're tearing down the iconic green.
Silent, the way I can't catch my breath, that panicked shut-valve,

this is how an island disappears, the square acre we made
our footholding: the used bookstore housing half our words,

the gas station too, the rectangle of sky above that opens like a rhombus,
the stumbled-upon pub's dented hardwood ostensible time capsule.

But today they're tearing down the Village pub where we said,
Disappear? I hear again the wind, again in the construction site.

It was a dark and stormy night; held semibreve on reed instrument.

It was staying awake until light; to have somewhere to return.

It was the sports field; so frozen it broke collarbones.

It was acquired behaviour; stacking wooden bricks high.

It was me; hurling a tennis racket into the court's tarmac.

It was glimpse and slipshod; learning in the aftermath.

It was texting back, *Actually, no; I don't believe you.*

It was me; not growing out of hurling a tennis racket into &c.

It was Florida daylight's refusal to acknowledge time passing; hover.

It was what could not be set aside; loyalest of memories.

It was each of you; your vectors those welcome infringements.

It was a dark and stormy night. We keep returning here, as if mocking what we saw gather from nowhere we least expected it isn't enough. *Grief-raft:* it's not your phrase yet I wish you knew that when I hear it in others' mouths I think of seven-year-old you as your parents board their house in Florida shutters, your closed eyes trying to will away whatever weather hurricanes your way. How crying is an act of drowning out—a way to lose oneself without being lost to something else. This is not my memory and I do not know how to tell you what it means to me, or if you mind my telling it here to others. These are recursions, cursory attempts to realise that what we haven't shared connects us as much or more than what I wish we had. That these weathered days I'm in conversation with you all even from as far away as here where telescopes are out of reach beyond the radar's ken. What I meant to say was that you should think of these not as poems but postcards: wish you where. Here I am, after you telling me about the aftereffects of storm, the dark spaces that inhabit you. When I'm not writing you, my fingers bind together a small vessel of ice-cream sticks, twined into a raft. In one version of these postcards, our daughters float them on whichever puddles weather throws up. In another, these are the forgotten bric-a-brac of our lives approaching and retreating. It was a dark and stormy night; how it continued I don't yet know.

Too easy for it to have been dark, or stormy, or blizzard
again or frog-rain, locust-wind, any handed-down sign
of the out-of-kilter. We've been talking of marathons

as though we've erased their martial routes, as if delivery
had always been our purpose. How marathon
                                                                    signals

what the human form attains at its limits where skin
is most haptic. When you say marathon
                                                            I hear adrenalin,

how it triggers enough blood to the hands and feet
to lift a car. When you say marathon
                                                    it means the body

external doesn't matter: what's muscular is the oxygen
we can't ever quite touch. I'll take that. I'll hear
marathon
                        and might think shrapnel, the outward
shape of glass distracted from looking in, percussion
toppling the human form at the limbs, ghosted
by past explosions, and when you say marathon

I'll think we don't know what within the body
touches the outside world, nudges its axis. When
you say marathon, we'll hear continuation. We'll trust
you're out there at the cusp of arrival, distance
what the blood maps—we just its seismographs.
Again you say marathon, and something courses.

It was a dark and stormy night, though if
I don't keep saying that I am forgotten,
tell me what's next. The roadway's trees

stencilled in only, flickering. I'd kept you
out into rain. I'd yet to learn that giving
may be the way we surrender ourselves

from things, not what we're seen to bestow.
That I couldn't bring with me the sights
of land I'd overflown, the way I'd avenued

these streets before you were here. Emerson
advises we call upon each other with only
what's perishable—flowers, fruit, seed—

and therefore replenished. I have as few
organic things to offer as the gifts I owe:
the indoor citrus tree, the driftwood

plinth, the composter. All the while
the radar whirrs, spinning into distance.
If we lock the door and simply don't return

we might never have to wonder whether
we needed the radar in the first place
but won't ever know if the citrus survived,

its limes data we've been too busy to read.

It was a dark and stormy night; but who remembers
the rest of Bulwer-Lytton's sentence, what happens
after the semi-colon's hinge: the rain's exceptions
and occasional intervals, that having left us lightless
and swept us up the streets alongside the contention
of lamplight the novel's opening ends in darkness?

I want to say that in that first sentence I become
the wind in the streets: what makes air shift
escapes me yet here I'm hurried along towards
the fountains that geyser in pedestrian squares,
some stirring of divination. In that sentence
the wind's perspective, or how tonight I've seen

too much of what I've left behind and not enough
of what I thought I could freight into today. As if
sometimes it is a dark and stormy night yet still
I want to apologise for this. Yes, and sorry, and if
we were now to meet across the cracked spines
of books would we have edited the intervening

and what led us here? It was a dark and stormy
night and then it isn't. I hadn't realised I
passing through might not ever be returning.

Acknowledgements

[It was in the absence of light] was previously published, under the title Radar Data #12, as "Poem-a-Day" at the Academy of American Poets on October 10, 2013.

"[It was a dark and stormy night. It was rainy weather]" and "[It was a dark and stormy night. Night an approximation]" are forthcoming in the journal English.

"[It was a dark and stormy night. We keep returning here, as if]" owes a debt to the poetry of Chelsea Rathburn.

The writing of these poems was made possible in part by funding from SUNY Geneseo's Provost's Office and the SUNY Research Foundation.

My Radar Data Knows Its Thing is an anagram attributed to Keith Knight. This chapbook is for my friends, who have crossed distance with me more than enough, and Jess especially.